WITHDRAWN

WE'VE MINDS OF OUR OWN

and

NINE FLOORS, NOT COUNTING THE MEZZANINE

Two Short Plays

by

WILLIAM NORFOLK

SAMUEL   FRENCH

LONDON

SAMUEL FRENCH LTD
26 SOUTHAMPTON STREET, STRAND, LONDON

SAMUEL FRENCH INC
25 WEST 45TH STREET, NEW YORK
7623 SUNSET BOULEVARD, HOLLYWOOD

SAMUEL FRENCH (CANADA) LTD
27 GRENVILLE STREET, TORONTO

SAMUEL FRENCH (AUSTRALIA) PTY LTD
ELIZABETHAN THEATRE TRUST BUILDING
153 DOWLING STREET, SYDNEY

MADE AND PRINTED IN GREAT BRITAIN BY
LATIMER, TREND AND CO. LTD, PLYMOUTH

MADE IN ENGLAND

WE'VE MINDS OF OUR OWN

First presented by Stephen Joseph's Studio Theatre Company at the Library Theatre, Scarborough, on the 9th September 1961, with the following cast of characters:

(in the order of their appearance)

FLO	*Rosamund Dickson*
AGGIE	*Hazel Burt*

WE'VE MINDS OF OUR OWN

Scene—*A mountain top.*

When the Curtain *rises, two women,* Aggie *and* Flo *sit at the top of the mountain. They are strangers.* Aggie *coughs.*

Flo. Pardon?

Aggie. I didn't speak.

Flo. I thought not.

(Aggie *pauses for a moment while she thinks*)

Aggie. Then why did you say "pardon"?

Flo. Pardon?

Aggie. There! You said it again! I asked why you said "pardon". If you didn't think I spoke.

Flo. But you *did* speak!

Aggie. I didn't!

Flo. Then why did I say pardon? I can assure you I don't go around saying pardon to every stranger I happen to meet on a mountain!

Aggie. Perhaps you *thought* you heard me?

Flo. Heard you what?

Aggie. Say something.

Flo. Why should I say something? I don't even know you. And you've got a tongue in your head, haven't you? *You* say something!

Aggie. I'm Aggie. Short for Agnes.

Flo. That's nice. I'm Flo. Short for Florence. Like the city. And Florence Nightingale. My aunt was a Florence, too.

Aggie. Was she now? Fancy!

Flo. Florence Matilda Persephone Mudlark. That was my aunt. I'm Florence Matilda *Terpsichore* Mudlark.

(Aggie *smiles and twiddles her thumbs. Suddenly her face becomes illuminated*)

Aggie. Have you got a telly?

FLO. No.

AGGIE. I have. (*Pause*) A *square* one. (*Pause*) So educational. Did you know there was such a bird as a genet? Or that only one hundred and fifty spotted shark whales have ever been recorded?

FLO. No.

AGGIE. Nor did I.

FLO. What do you mean by "recorded"? Do they make a noise?

AGGIE. They didn't say.

FLO. Oh.

AGGIE. It's so useful to know things. (*Pause*) Are you sure you haven't got a telly?

FLO. Quite sure.

AGGIE. That's funny.

FLO. What is?

AGGIE. Not having a telly. It must be like not having running water, or a lavatory. If I had my way they'd be built into houses, like fireplaces. For instance, I was watching a programme the other week—and do you know what? All the people in the world could be got into a box half a mile square!

FLO. Fancy!

AGGIE. Is that educational, or isn't it?

FLO. Oh, I've been told how educational it is. Full of really useful information, so my neighbour tells me.

AGGIE. Half a mile square! I wonder how *they* know?

FLO. Experimented with dummies, I expect.

AGGIE. Of course, it would be a bit of a squash.

FLO. I dare say.

AGGIE. And uncomfortable for them at the bottom.

(*Pause*)

FLO. What sort of a box? Did *they* say?

AGGIE. A square one, I expect. Most boxes are square.

FLO. Boot boxes aren't. Not unless your feet are as broad as they're long. Nor are hat-boxes, nor match-boxes, nor cigarette-boxes, nor . . .

AGGIE. I meant *square* boxes.

FLO. There's no need to get all upset about it. Besides,

that's not what I meant. I meant what was the box *made* of?

AGGIE. *They* didn't say.

FLO. Now that *does* surprise me. I should have thought that was the most important thing.

AGGIE. I must say that I don't really see the point of it.

FLO. They do some pretty pointless things.

AGGIE. And, furthermore, this box could be dropped into the Grand Canyon, and lost from sight.

FLO. Why the Grand Canyon, I wonder? Why not the Cheddar Gorge, or somewhere in the Pennines?

AGGIE. Because the Grand Canyon's more *central*, I suppose.

FLO. More central to what?

AGGIE. Wherever the box is, I expect.

FLO. Well, I'll tell you one thing. They'll never get me into no such box. I'd *die* first!

AGGIE. Well, dear, *they* weren't actually talking of *doing* it. I think.

FLO. Ah, that's the cunning of it. They've only mentioned it at first. Put out a fly feeler, as it were. But now that the idea's there it's only a matter of time before someone votes *them* into power, and they try it.

AGGIE. Oh, I hope not. I'm claustrophobic!

FLO. But forewarned is forearmed. Now that we know of the plot we'll be wary if ever *they* ask us to build *them* a box half a mile square, and we'll *strike!*

AGGIE. Of course, I suppose I'd get used to it in time.

FLO. You infuriate me, Aggie. Here you are, letting yourself be sat on . . .

AGGIE. We'll all be sat on! And trodden on! And jumped on! Do you think it will be air-conditioned?

FLO. Cheer up! It may never happen!

AGGIE. I wonder how long it will be for? Besides, I don't know anyone in Grand Canyon. It's cruel, that's what it is. Putting us among a lot of strangers, whether we like it or not, and expecting us to be caged in the same box . . .

FLO. Personally, I like a change every now and then.

AGGIE. Supposing they lost the key, and we were locked in for ever? What then? I'll miss my little bed. And I don't know what my husband's going to say when I tell him we're moving to Grand Canyon.

FLO. Well, what's got to be's got to be, and there's nothing we can do but make the best of it. I'll get there late, I think, and make sure I'm not shoved at the bottom.

AGGIE. I do hope there are separate compartments for men and women. To put us together would be—*indecent!*

FLO. I shouldn't think there'd be *room* to be indecent.

AGGIE. Though I don't think I'd mind even that, so long as I'm allowed to take my summer dresses. It's bound to be very hot.

FLO. Oh, I don't think we'll be allowed *clothes*. They'd take up room!

AGGIE. You mean we're all to be *naked* . . . ! Did *they* say when we're to go?

FLO. No, but I think it's pretty soon. You see, the world's population is increasing, and if *they* don't send us soon *they'll* never get us all into a box that size. *They'll* have to do it quickly, for economy reasons.

FLO. And if it's got to be a *square* box, just think of the awkwardness of making it bigger. It has to be more each way, if you see what I mean. And perhaps the extra number of people wouldn't quite fit, and *they'd* be chopping lumps off, and sticking lumps on, and . . .

AGGIE. Off the *people?*

FLO. No. The box. *They'll* stand on top pressing a few hundred more in with their feet, like grape-crushers, and all the time *they'll* be becoming more and more convinced that *they'll* never make it. It'll be like packing a suit-case, you mark my words. *They'll* be putting us in, taking us out, rearranging us, putting us this way and that way, folding us in the middle, curling us into little balls, crushing us into little heaps, putting us head to feet, and at the end of it all we'll have to come out and be put into a bigger box. No-one's messing me about like that. After all, I'm not as young as I was. (*Pause*) Where is this Grand Canyon?

AGGIE. They didn't say on the telly. China, I believe.

FLO. It'll be a jade box, or ivory, you mark my words!

AGGIE. Fancy.

FLO. Yes. Very fancy, I should think. *Carved!* Though, to tell you the truth, I never really cared for jade. Cut glass has such a *sparkle.*

AGGIE. Well, I'm glad it's not going to be *wood!*

FLO. Why?

AGGIE. *Woodworm!* It would be hell. I'd be lying there itching to get at them with a good dose of D.D.T., but unable to move hand or foot while they crunched away to their hearts' content. Then, of course, there's the death-watch beetle . . .

FLO. On the other hand, perhaps it won't be jade. They won't spend that much on us. After all, we're only working class . . .

AGGIE. With a capital WC. I wonder what *they'll* do with the box when we've been scraped out of it?

FLO. Sell it to America?

AGGIE. Shouldn't think they'd want it. They've already got the Empire State Building.

FLO. They'll chop it up and make things out of it.

AGGIE. You mean souvenirs?

FLO. Yes. Paper knives, and things.

AGGIE. That would be nice. We could keep happy little memories of this historic occasion.

FLO. That's right.

AGGIE. Is it an historic occasion?

FLO. Well, we've never done it before, have we?

AGGIE. No.

FLO. Then it must be historic.

AGGIE. But it's going to be uncomfortable.

FLO. Oh, you make me lose patience! You're never satisfied!

AGGIE. Oh, I'm not meaning . . .

FLO. Yes, you are! They give you a free trip to Grand Canyon, even find you accommodation, and you sit there grousing about discomfort. You shouldn't be given such golden opportunities!

AGGIE. I deserve them as much as you, and if you think I'm being left out you've got another think coming!

FLO. Just imagine it! Lying there in a box, with nothing

to do. No housework, no cooking, no shopping. Whoever dreamed it up deserves a medal!

AGGIE. Just let me find I'm not down to go and I'll want to know why!

FLO. It'll probably be on a "first-come-first-served" basis, and the last to apply might as well save themselves the bother!

AGGIE. If I'm left out I'll die! I can just see my neighbours, particularly old mother Pippit, poking their heads over the top of the box and sniggering at me as I'm turned away. I'd never be able to lift my head again.

FLO. That settles it! I'm going to see about my ticket *now!*

AGGIE. Me, too. Where do we go?

FLO. A Labour Exchange, I should think. After all, we've been promised a place in the box, and it's our right to clamp down on *them* and demand it.

AGGIE. And if *they* think *they* can turn us away now that we're looking forward to it, they're mistaken!

FLO. The cheek of it! First of all telling us we can go, then changing *their* minds. They think *they* can do what *they* like with us, that's the trouble!

AGGIE. You're so right! Well, we'll show *them* we've got minds of our own!

(AGGIE and FLO *prepare to leave*)

I can't wait to see the look on *their* faces when *they* find the box is too small . . .

AGGIE and FLO *exit in high dudgeon as—*

the CURTAIN *falls*

LIGHTING PLOT

Property fittings required: none

Exterior. The same scene throughout

THE MAIN ACTING AREA is a place C stage which represents the mountain top

To open: Effect of daylight on the mountain top

No cues

NINE FLOORS, NOT COUNTING THE MEZZANINE

First presented by Stephen Joseph's Studio Theatre Company at the London Welsh Hall, Gray's Inn Road, London, on the 8th November 1961, with the following cast of characters:

(in the order of their appearance)

MADAME RENE	*Patricia England*
MILLIE RAISIN	*Hazel Burt*
SIMON PORTER	*Richard Gill*

The action of the Play passes in the "studio" of Madame Rene

Time—the Present

NINE FLOORS, NOT COUNTING THE MEZZANINE

SCENE—*The "studio" of Madame Rene.*

It is is a colourful, chaotic room, filled with astrological charts, devil-masks and such paraphernalia as the occupier feels necessary to impress her clients. The overall effect is dramatic and somewhat unreal. There is a fireplace in the R wall, a window C back which is shrouded in heavy curtains and a door L. There is a small table before the window, another small table below the fireplace on which there is a gramophone and a larger table RC. This table is covered with a chenille or velveteen cloth and on the cloth reposes a crystal ball. There are upright chairs R, L and above this table. There is an armchair above the fireplace and other upright chairs below the door and L of the window. Other suitable dressing may be added at the discretion of the Producer.

When the CURTAIN *rises,* MADAME RENE *is dancing about to a recording of Afro-Cuban jazz which is playing on the gramophone. She tries on various costumes which are lying about on the chairs—each one decorated with symbols, some meaningless, but all very impressive. Her secretary-cum-friend,* MILLIE RAISIN, *enters. She doesn't believe in Madame's powers.* MADAME *ceases her dance and stops the gramophone.*

MILLIE. Are you planning a soubrette speciality to liven up the act?

MADAME. I do wish you wouldn't refer to my consultations as "the act"!

MILLIE. Why not? It's all a load of rubbish! You know it, and I know it, so why pretend to each other that there's more to it than that? Madame Rene! Don't forget, love, that you're still Bessie Brasher to me!

MADAME. I simply couldn't bill myself as "Bessie Brasher —High Priestess of the Occult", could I, Millie? Besides—

let's face it—I'm not a Bessie Brasher. As a matter of fact, I'm inclined to think that no-one could possibly be.

MILLIE. I'm not so sure about that. Sometimes you're definitely leaning toward Brasher—the old Bessie, machining bra-straps down at Levy's.

MADAME. Being a High Priestess is more lucrative, and employs my natural talents. Besides, don't you think it's a sort of—progression?

MILLIE. From the uplifting of pendulous bosoms to the uplifting of pendulous souls? Not really. Very noble, I'm sure, but at least we were once able to see the result of your work!

MADAME. Do you think purple for this afternoon's client?

MILLIE. I'd say a sort of muddy-grey. That's the impression he gives. He's thin, bespectacled, drear, and probably has a wife who doesn't understand him.

MADAME. Perhaps something a bit more maternal?

MILLIE. Yes. Like a flowered pinny, and a sloppy pair of worn-out carpet slippers. Maybe a scruffy bun at the nape of the neck. I think . . .

MADAME. Sometimes I wish you'd think more *silently!*

MILLIE. Once I've thought it, I have to say it. I get a sort of compulsion.

MADAME. Did he say what he wanted? A seance? His fortune read? Advice?

MILLIE. He read the board outside, and said, "I'll start off with a consultation, because that's the cheapest."

MADAME. Did he sound—regretful?

MILLIE. He sounded exactly as though he was ordering bread and butter because the rest of the menu was too steep.

MADAME. I mean, did he sound as though he'd like—for instance—a seance, if he could afford it?

MILLIE. I'm not psychic. If I were, I'd open up a rival establishment. Sorry. I forgot you don't like the place being called that. Why do you ask?

MADAME. I feel in the mood for a seance. Something long and exhausting. There's been so much routine stuff this week.

MILLIE. If you feel in the mood for a seance, I've no

doubt you'll persuade him he needs one. The customer's always right because you've always sold him exactly what you wanted to sell.

MADAME. That remark is both grammatically and factually incorrect!

MILLIE. The sentiment's correct enough!

MADAME. How you can possibly doubt my powers beats me! You've seen me in action!

MILLIE. An unfortunate word—action! I've seen you standing like a sleepwalker, gurgling.

MADAME (*anxiously*) But not in my own voice?

MILLIE. I've never heard you gurgling in any other voice.

MADAME. I wasn't gurgling.

MILLIE. How do you know, if you were in a trance?

MADAME. I don't completely lose consciousness.

MILLIE. You stay just conscious enough to see if your audience is impressed?

MADAME. Does nothing impress *you*?

MILLIE. Yes. People's gullibility. They come in here, you peddle them a few second-hand dreams, and they really believe this "High Priestess" lark. They don't even question why Madame Rene should have the accent of a shoe-shop assistant!

MADAME. They probably prefer to imagine. That way they can make me into a Rumanian princess, stolen, as a child, by gipsies.

MILLIE. Where's the point? It's not true.

MADAME. Don't split hairs. You should have been an analyst.

MILLIE. Looking at things under microscopes? No. I prefer to see things in correct proportion.

MADAME. Some people prefer not to see them at all. So they come to me. Who can blame them? What's so wrong about selling illusions? It happens every day. The woman who buys the dress she's seen in a window buys the perverted illusion that she'll look like a chalk model. *Chacun à son goût!*

MILLIE. What absolute nonsense you talk, Bessie!

MADAME. And don't call me Bessie!

MILLIE. You could have called yourself "Madame Bessie", I suppose. I agree that it doesn't sound continental. Some day, you know, you're going to get a Frenchman in here, and then you'll be up to the neck in it, won't you? You can't keep a whole conversation going on *"chacun à son goût"*, and *"enfant terrible"*, you know. I only hope I'm here when it happens. If you'd pretended to be Swahili, now that would have been safer. Something with a ring to it! Something like—"Bhowani Bessie".

MADAME. If you've quite finished amusing yourself, Millie Raisin . . .

MILLIE. Nearly, Bess. How would you like me to give you real class by calling myself Señorita Carmen?

MADAME. Millie Raisin is quite distinctive enough, thank you! And now, perhaps you'd go and keep an eye open for the client, if your vaudeville turn is over.

MILLIE. Well, of course, if that's how you feel . . . (*She turns to go*)

MADAME. By the way, what's the name of the client?

MILLIE. Porter. Simon Porter.

(MILLIE *goes out.* MADAME *starts the jazz record again, resumes her dancing, and settles for a kimono-type wrap in scarlet and black. After a moment a timid knock is heard.* MADAME *doesn't hear it. It is repeated.* MADAME *quickly arranges herself into an over-dramatic pose, before she answers*)

MADAME. *Entrez!*

(SIMON PORTER *enters. He has been adequately described by Millie. He stands shyly awaiting a word from Madame*)

Do come in and make yourself comfortable. I am Madame Rene: palmist, spiritualist, professional confidante—phrenologist, astrologist, occasional witch. In which capacity do you wish to consult me? (*She moves to the gramophone and stops it*)

SIMON. I wish to contact my son.

MADAME. He is no longer with us?

SIMON. No. He's dead.

MADAME. Do sit down,

(SIMON *does so*)

That is to say, he has passed over. We don't die. The fee is one guinea, payable in advance. The charge includes the expense of such other of my capacities as are found necessary . . . I understand it *is* a consultation you require? For another seven and six I could arrange a small seance . . .

SIMON. No, thank you. (*He gives her some money*) I really want advice.

MADAME. You look a deserving case. Perhaps I will throw in a little seance—*free!* You have a very interesting head . . .

SIMON. About my son . . .

MADAME. Let us not be impatient. It's not like picking up a telephone. Would you please hand me a personal object. It helps me to "tune in", as it were.

SIMON. He was murdered.

MADAME. Please don't tell me about him. Give me time, and I'll tell *you*.

SIMON. Pushed down a lift-shaft.

MADAME. Really, Mr Porter!

SIMON. Some drunken American sailors did it.

MADAME (*resignedly*) He was your only son?

SIMON. I tried to tell the police, but they wouldn't listen.

MADAME. Are you sure you wouldn't like a seance?

SIMON. Sometimes, of an evening, I play *Abide with Me* on the harmonium, and I feel him in the room with me. He tried to talk, lots of times, but he can't.

MADAME. Ah, that's because you haven't the *power!* Now perhaps I could help . . .

SIMON. Polly doesn't believe I have a son.

MADAME. You're making things terribly difficult, you know. If only you'd stop talking for a moment, I . . .

SIMON. She runs away from reality. It's her main fault. Polly's not his mother, you understand. Polly's my second wife, as it were. If I'd married either of them that is. Nancy was his mother. *You* believe me, don't you?

MADAME. Would you like me to speak to him?

SIMON. Can you make him speak to me?

MADAME. You won't hear him, but I will.

SIMON. Why should he speak to you, a complete stranger? He was always shy with strangers.

MADAME. Circumstances are somewhat different now.

SIMON. I want to know why he was pushed. Nine floors, not counting the mezzanine.

MADAME. What will you do if you find out?

SIMON. I'll *know!*

(MADAME *sits very erect in her chair and appears to be intently listening for something*)

MADAME. I think I'm . . . Yes? . . . *Oui?* . . . *C'est Hortense?* . . . *Bonjour* . . . Would you repeat that? . . . *Oui!* . . . How many letters, *cheri?* . . . His name? . . . You know it? . . . *Oui!* . . . His name's——

SIMON. —George. I wanted to call him Peter, but Nancy persisted.

MADAME. Mr Porter! Are you deliberately trying to scorn my powers?

SIMON. It's very nice to have power. I wish I had more. It's super-persuasion. People *have* to believe you.

MADAME. Do people not believe you?

SIMON. Polly doesn't.

MADAME. Why not?

SIMON. She runs away from reality. She doesn't *want* to believe. And she doesn't want to believe in George because he doesn't belong to her. She wants me for herself.

MADAME (*suddenly*) Do you believe in potions?

SIMON. Not really.

MADAME. Then I won't waste time brewing one. They're quite harmless, of course. A bay leaf, snails from *Fortnums*, sherbert for fizz, a lacing of rum, and so forth. But if you don't believe in them it would be a waste of time. Some people swear by them.

SIMON. She didn't always want me for herself. At one time she told me to go out and meet people. "Make friends," she said. "You're too much on your own." And I did. But none of them were real. I got to know three Adamses, two Atkinsons, four Bloggs, nine Browns, one Charlesworth, five Dennisses, twelve Evanses, two Forsters, ten Fosters, twenty-seven Greens . . .

MADAME. Yes, this is all very interesting. But where does it get us?

SIMON. One of the Adamses lived at forty-two Shakespeare Road, Peckham. Another lived in Cheyne Walk, Chelsea. The other was from Manor Road, West Ham. The Atkinsons . . .

MADAME. Yes, but . . .

SIMON. How can you help me if you won't even listen? *None of them were real, I tell you!* They were flesh and blood, but not *real!*

MADAME. But how can I help?

SIMON. Bring George back. I've lost him.

MADAME. I've been trying to bring him back, but you . . .

SIMON. Make him tell me why . . .

MADAME (*shouting him down*) Don't interrupt! And stop taking for granted that I'm a wailing-wall! George was your son, by Nancy?

SIMON. Yes, and he . . .

MADAME. "Yes" will do. And Polly doesn't believe in him?

SIMON. That's right. She says . . .

MADAME. What happened to Nancy?

SIMON. She went away. George was all I had left. He . . .

MADAME. Why did she go away?

SIMON. I got rid of her.

MADAME. Why?

SIMON. I didn't need her. I had George.

MADAME. And George was pushed down a lift-shaft?

SIMON. Yes. Nine floors, not counting . . .

MADAME. I imagine no-one *was* counting, under the circumstances. Five, including the mezzanine, would probably have done as well.

SIMON (*glaring at her*) It's not a joke, you know!

MADAME. You surprise me!

SIMON. After all, I've paid a guinea to bring him back!

MADAME. Which is very cheap for a return ticket from—wherever he is. How old was he?

SIMON. Twenty-five. That is to say, twenty-four years, three months, two weeks, four . . .

MADAME. We'll dispense with the odd minutes. I prefer round figures. And how long ago did this event occur?

SIMON. Twenty-eight years ago. That is to say, twenty-seven . . .

MADAME. Twenty-eight will do! (*She frowns*) And how old are you?

SIMON. What has that to do with it?

MADAME. Mere curiosity.

SIMON. Work it out for yourself. I was nearly fifty when he was born. I think that's why I was so fond of the lad. He came at the end of a late summer.

MADAME (*after a slight calculation*) That makes you a hundred and three?

SIMON. Does it? Doesn't time fly? Well? Where is he?

MADAME. Why didn't Nancy believe in him?

SIMON. She said she couldn't see it. If she'd had a son she said she thought she would have known about it. It's these twilight sleeps. They're walking around one minute, thinking they're putting on weight, and the next minute they're in a dream, and when they come out of it, it's all over. So I said she'd probably mislaid him, and forgot about him, because he was there all right.

MADAME. And what did she say?

SIMON. She said it was imagination. When I was sitting talking to him, she used to sit in the chair—on his lap!—and say, "There's no-one there. Now will you believe me?" She was always doing that. One day, when she got up, he was gone. I don't know how he managed it, 'cos she was a fair size. Then he stayed away for a while. I asked him why, and he said he was tired of getting sat on. So she had to go.

MADAME. So you told her to leave?

SIMON. I couldn't do that. After all, she was his mother. I couldn't have her walking the streets.

MADAME. So what did you do?

SIMON. I killed her. She was never real anyway. But the day I did it, George fell down the lift-shaft. Or, that is to say, he was pushed down nine floors . . .

MADAME. Not counting the mezzanine. And you've been trying to see him ever since?

SIMON. I know he'd be glad to see me. We understand each other. Do you always take this long? After all, you're a High Priestess.

MADAME. You don't become a High Priestess for doing a four-minute mile!

SIMON. Can't you get that little French bit to get a move on?

MADAME. Hortense? (*She suddenly jerks*) Ouch! I'm sorry, *cheri*. (*To Simon*) She objects to being called "a little French bit". What's that, *cheri?* . . . No! He said "bit"! B-I-T!

SIMON. Tell her his name's George.

MADAME. We know that, Mr Porter, but I don't think we can help you.

SIMON. Why not?

MADAME. Well—er—it was a long time ago. And—er . . .

SIMON. So?

MADAME. And—he doesn't seem to be there.

SIMON (*ugly*) You don't believe in him, either, do you?

MADAME. Of course . . .

SIMON. You don't. I can see it in your eyes. You're just like the rest of 'em. Faced with reality, you turn and run a mile. You're afraid of reality, aren't you? Because it'll show you for the sham that you are. That everyone is. That's why they all run from it!

MADAME (*escaping*) I'll just consult my assistant, Miss Raisin. She may be able to help. She's—er—she's . . .

(*Lost for words,* MADAME *flies from the room. Alone,* SIMON *looks about him, nervously. Suddenly his eyes focus on a spot, and follow an imaginary movement*)

SIMON. George! You are here! She said she couldn't contact you. (*He listens*) No, you've never seen a room like this before. They just don't exist, except in the imagination. (*He listens*) You think she's gone—for the police? (*He listens*) But why? (*He listens*) Because of Nancy? (*He listens*) Because I killed her? But that's nothing to do with this High Priestess. Besides, Nancy was only a figment of the imagination, dressed up in shapeless flesh. She . . . (*He *listens*) They'll never destroy you, George. Nancy tried, and so did Polly. But you're still here. This woman can't do it. She's tried, but she won't succeed because we're stronger than she is. We proved that, didn't we? Nancy! Polly! (*He listens*) You think that? You think she'll keep me talking until the police arrive? (*He listens*) No. I won't tell her you were here, so she won't guess that you've warned me. (*He listens*) Till tomorrow, then. Good-bye, son. Take care of yourself. (*He sits at the table as though nothing has happened*)

(MADAME *enters*)

MADAME. She's not there!

SIMON. Who's not there?

MADAME. My assistant, Millie Raisin.

SIMON. Millie Raisin?

MADAME. Yes.

SIMON. *Raisin?*

MADAME (*impatiently*) Yes. Like one puts in cakes!

SIMON. An unlikely name, that! Raisin!

MADAME. I believe she stays single, just to keep it.

SIMON. Who is this unlikely woman?

MADAME. My assistant.

SIMON. Then why isn't she assisting you?

MADAME. She does. She acts as my secretary. You made your appointment with her.

SIMON. I didn't make no appointment with no Millie Raisin!

MADAME. Of course you did! She's—well, large—and has—sort of—mauve hair.

SIMON. *Mauve* hair?

MADAME. And one or two gold teeth.

SIMON. You're having me on!

MADAME. Mr Porter! I most certainly am not "having you on"!

SIMON. Mauve hair—gold teeth—Millie Raisin . . . She *can't* be real!

MADAME. Now you come to mention it . . .

SIMON (*rising*) Show her to me!

MADAME. I tell you I can't find her. (*She goes to the door and calls*) Millie!

(*There is no reply*)

Millie! (*To Simon*) You *must* have seen her.

SIMON. I haven't. If she's real, show her to me. Go on! Show her to me!

MADAME. How can I, if she's not there?

SIMON. As soon as you mentioned the name I was suspicious. I've met all kinds of names in my time, but never that one. Iggletrump—Goggerpicket—Fiddlewomper —but never a Millie Raisin!

MADAME. But you've *met* her! Only this . . .

SIMON. I don't know what you're up to, but I don't like it! (*Sidling to the door*) I'll call back, I think—when—er— yes, when . . . There's something mad going on . . . (*He has reached the door*) Millie Raisin!

SIMON *shrieks with laughter, and runs off.* MADAME *sits at the table, amazed at the turn of events. Her arm brushes the crystal ball, which falls to the ground, and shatters as—*

the CURTAIN *falls*

FURNITURE AND PROPERTY PLOT

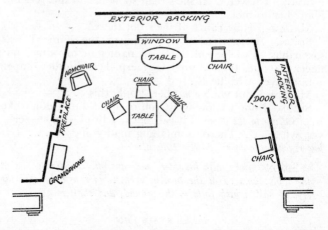

On stage: 5 upright chairs. *Scattered over them:* weird costumes covered in cabalistic symbols

Armchair. *On it:* scarlet and black kimono-type wrap

Small table down R. *On it:* gramophone. *On gramophone:* Afro-Cuban jazz record

Small table up C

Table C. *On it:* velveteen or chenille cloth, crystal ball

Heavy curtains for window

Astrological charts, devil-masks, etc.

Personal: SIMON: assorted money in his pocket

LIGHTING PLOT

Property fittings required: none

Interior. The same scene throughout

THE MAIN ACTING AREAS are R, at a table C and LC

To open: Effect of general interior light
Curtains drawn over the window